GRATITUDE

Gratitude

Creating a Happier You

STEPHANIE RICHEY

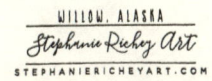

Stephanie Richey Art

Contents

1	Introduction	1
2	Intellectual	3
3	Nature	8
4	People	13
5	Physical	18
6	Spiritual	23
7	Talents	28
8	Keep Going	33
About Me		43

Copyright © 2021 by Stephanie Richey

All rights reserved. No part of this book may be reproduced in any manner whatsoever without written permission except in the case of brief quotations embodied in critical articles and reviews.

First Printing, 2021

Chapter 1

Introduction

I wrote this book as a reminder to me, and hopefully a help for others, to begin the process of, or remind ourselves of, the things we have in life to be grateful for. There is so much in life to be grateful for. Gratitude changes our attitude, and helps us focus on the good in life. Gratitude lifts us above the problems in life and helps us find solutions. Gratitude helps us see all that is good in our lives and turns our attention to those things, rather than the hard and bad. Not that those things don't exist, but often when we can look back and see the good, the hard and bad don't seem quite as big. Instead, we are able to look ahead at solutions, or at least see that we have conquered so much, so we can keep conquering. I hope you will use this book as a work book, but as a beginning or middle, not an end. Being grateful is a lifelong pursuit.

Throughout this book I will talk about 6 areas of gratitude. Obviously, there are way more areas, but this will hopefully help you get started on your journey to being more grateful. I know it has helped me as I have written it. At the end of this book, I will have the categories listed again with space to continue writing. You may fill these pages as your read this book, or it may take you weeks, months or years to complete all the spaces of all, or one particular area. You may also decide to create your own book for those things you are grateful for and not use any of the spaces provided. The goal is to help you get started on a lifelong path of being grateful. Whether you've been on this path of gratitude your whole life already, or are just starting out, I hope this book helps you move forward with new insights, and new ideas or ways to have gratitude every day.

Chapter 2

Intellectual

I am grateful for the ability to learn. There are so many options out there now that give us ample opportunity to learn anything from simple, non-degree things like how to cook, how to sew, how to paint, etc., to more complex things that require college degrees -- a lot of which you can do at home now rather than having to attend a college or university in person. I am grateful for the opportunities I have taken to learn things that have benefitted my life. I will share a few with you. Think about ways in which your education has blessed your life, or ways in which you have been educated that you are grateful for.

When my kids were little, I wanted to learn how to sew better. I thought at one point I wanted to be a seamstress for a living. I wanted to learn basic sewing principles and techniques as well as how to make my own patterns. I looked online and found a course offered through a university in Arizona. The class was in hard copy book form for the majority of the work, the tests were given online. The final was submitted through the mail in picture form. It was a good class. The things I learned in this class allowed me to make my daughters some dresses completely from scratch, I made so many shorts for all my kids, as well as pajama pants and fleece jackets. I still make my own dresses and on occasion I make skirts, pants, and jackets for myself as well. The things I learned in that class have stuck with me, and I am grateful for the knowledge that I gained.

I love to cook, but I haven't always liked to eat super healthy. When I started to get in better shape, I decided I needed to learn to cook better so that I could make healthier meals for our family, as well as make things taste good. I didn't take online or book courses for this, I decided there was enough free information just on the TV. I love watching cooking shows, and shows like America's Test Kitchen and Cooks Country were really great helps. I liked those as well, because they had the science behind why things worked and why they tasted better. I'm definitely not a gourmet cook, but as I watched those shows with the intent to understand and apply what I was learning, my ability to make better tasting food increased, and the kids now say that I am a good cook and they like almost everything I make. I also like that we eat a lot healthier when I cook at home as compared to fast food or boxed foods. Now, there are so many videos online with recipes that make finding good, healthy food recipes easy, and make learning how to cook easy and inexpensive. I am grateful for these free options.

Painting is a new found love of mine. New as in the last 6 or 7 years. This was not something even on my radar until I took my daughters to an art class offered by a friend. They came home with some awesome art that I decided I wanted to try. The art teacher created a series of lessons online called Createful Christmas (www.createfulart.com) and I decided to try it. Fortunately, they turned out fairly good initially, because I liked it and kept going. I decided I liked watercolor more than acrylics so I started to search the internet for online courses. There, I found, are a ton of free courses. I also picked up books about watercolor techniques at the library and our local bookstores. I have learned so much, but I think the thing I love about painting more than anything, is how relaxing it is for me. I can be up-tight and frustrated with life and sit down and paint, and it all just melts away. I am grateful for that initial class my kids took and the inspiration it was to me, to try something new.

This one may sound funny, because it is not my profession, nor do I necessarily use it every day. But I am grateful for the education I have gotten working with my husband. He builds custom homes for a living. I worked with him every day for the first five years of our marriage as we didn't have any kids. I have learned so much about good foundations, which I have applied to so many aspects of my life, in setting goals and having priorities. Having that solid base is the most important part of a home, as well as a life. I have learned the importance of a good framework, and not cutting corners. The only thing we generally see when we purchase a home is the finishes. But just because something looks good on the outside doesn't mean that it was build correctly on the inside. So many times, my husband has come in after a different contractor to fix areas where corners were cut, some minor, some major structural issues. This has taught me that there are no shortcuts to true success. Just because it looks good on the outside doesn't mean that the inside was built right, and usually, it is in the times of challenge or struggle that we see if our own insides and foundation were built right or not. I am grateful for the lessons I've learned from building, as well as the confidence that if I ever needed to, I believe I could build a basic house without any additional instruction. This knowledge has also benefited me as I have built my own displays for my art shows.

There are so many opportunities to learn, every day. Education doesn't have to cost the earth. It is amazing to me the amount of helpful information that you can find in so many places, if you're willing to listen and learn. I am also grateful for the ability we have to learn, to think, and to reason. Learning is a lifelong pursuit that should never stop. If you feel stagnant in your life, learn something new. You never know where that education will take you.

Now it's your turn. What experiences have you had with gaining knowledge that have had an impact in your life. Big or small things can be pivotal in our lives, what knowledge have you gained that has altered the course of your life, or maybe even the course of your thoughts to become a better person? What is something you've learned today? Write down some of these educational experiences that you are grateful for below.

1._____

_____

2._____

_____

3._____

_____

GRATITUDE ~ 7

4._____

_____

5._____

_____

6._____

_____

7._____

_____

8._____

_____

9._____

_____

10._____

_____

Chapter 3

Nature

We live in a beautiful world. No matter where I go in this world there is something beautiful. The world around us was created for us, for our benefit and use. But the Lord didn't create it just to be a useful tool, He wanted us to be happy here, to find beauty in the world around us, to see the variety and realize that there are many different kinds of beauty.

I grew up in the desert southwest, in Southern Utah. Not much water, it seemed like we were always having a drought and having to conserve water. But the sage brush, I love the smell and color. The rocks and mountains, I love the red and orange, sometimes yellow and even white rocks found in that area, along with the white trunks of the aspen, the green leaves in the summer, and where I lived, it snowed in the winter. I loved every season. It was amazing what would grow there as well. We had a garden, as well as fruit trees, and my mom always has beautiful flowers around the house and yard. There is so much inspiration and peace there.

Now I live in Alaska, and there is beauty. Usually there is no worry about drought here, although we have had a few wildfires rip through our community in recent years. The trees are green all summer, so many trees. It rains regularly, and I don't know if it's from growing up in the desert or what, but I love the rain, I love the sound of rain, and I love the fresh smell of rain. In the winter, the snow is always fresh (because it snows a lot). When it gets really cold, the hoar frost is the most beautiful thing, it's like God dumped glitter, the perfect amount everywhere, and it just glistens. Looking out the windows during the day, there is always some sort of animal to see, whether its birds, fox, moose, or, on rare occasion a bear. It is beautiful!

I love hiking, biking, and exploring the world around me. Because of that I have had many experiences in nature that I am grateful for. I will share some here to get your thoughts moving. I want you to think and remember as I share some of my experiences, what are some from your life. You'll write them down in just a few minutes.

Growing up in the desert, everywhere was dry, so water is a premium, and any free-flowing water is fun to find and play in. In Southern Utah there is a place called Red Cliffs. It's not a huge tourist attraction like Zion or Arches National Park. Maybe that's why I loved it so much, not as many people. But it was a great place to hike and picnic. There is a small stream that ran through the area, down through the cliffs and across the road. I remember going there so many times as a family, playing in the water, and hiking through the cliffs and waterfalls. As a teenager, that is the first place that I went rappelling. I am grateful for the love I developed there of several things, exploring through hiking, playing in the water, and I am grateful for overcoming fear there. I wasn't afraid of heights ever that I can remember, but rappelling off a cliff, that takes a little more courage than just walking up next to the edge and walking away. I am grateful for those experiences.

When our kids were young, we went for a vacation down to visit family in Utah, and we went on a hike to Cascade Falls. I was hiking by my brother and we were talking about the trees. He told me to go smell one of the large pine trees. I thought he was being funny, but he said no, it smells like cinnamon. I didn't believe him, so I smelled the tree, and sure enough, the bark smelled like cinnamon. We always hear that we should stop and smell the roses, but how often do we stop and smell the trees? I am grateful for his invitation to smell the tree, and have done so on many occasions since then, not just in Utah. Most trees don't smell like cinnamon, but they do smell wonderful. I am grateful for the scent of nature.

My husband doesn't really like to hike. Plus, his job is more of a seasonal job, so he works all summer. But one summer I convinced him to go hiking with us. We went to Girdwood and hiked the Winner Creek Trail to a hand tram, and then back again. There was a lot of people at the hand tram when we got there, but we were usually alone on the trail. It was a wooded trail, peaceful and quiet most of the way. We listened to the birds and enjoyed all the old man's beard hanging from the trees. It felt like we had been transported to a different time. It was misty and cool, but not raining, and the sun did eventually come out. Everything was fresh and clean from the rain earlier and it was beautiful. I was grateful that day for the fresh green color that was so vibrant from the recent cleaning of the rain. As I have learned to paint, I see color differently, and I loved the color that day.

One year we went on a Fjords tour out of Seward. It was windy and raining when we were waiting for our boat, but when we got on the water, the rain stopped, and the ocean was calm. I have been on whale watching tours before, when we never saw anything, but not this trip. We saw whales, all around us. There were sea lions out sunning themselves near the shoreline. We saw puffins on the cliffs, flying around, and diving under the water. Jelly fish floating along just under the surface of the water. There was so much life out there. I was so grateful to be on that particular cruise (especially since I didn't get motion sick), and I am so grateful for the variety of animals that populate our earth. There is so much variety and beauty the Lord has blessed us with on this earth. I am grateful for the sea animals and birds that we saw that day.

I hope you have been thinking about experiences you have had out in nature. No matter where you live, city or country, desert or rainforest, or anything in between, there is beauty all around you. What are some things in nature that you are grateful for?

1._____

_____

2._____

_____

3._____

_____

4._____

_____

5.___

6.___

7.___

8.___

9.___

10.___

Chapter 4

People

There are so many people in our lives that have helped us. None of us are where we are all by ourselves. Good or bad we have been influenced by people around us, as we too influence others. It's important to see the people who have influenced us for the better and remember to be grateful for them, and if possible, to them directly. I have had many good influences in my life. I will tell you about a few of them. I hope as I share some of mine that you will think of and remember people in your life that have had an impact on you.

My parents. I know, most people are grateful for their parents, so you may wonder why that's on here because it seems generic, or it's so obvious. But literally, none of us would be here today without our parents. However, I was raised by good parents. I had a happy childhood. We weren't rich, and we weren't poor. We were part of the middle class. If ever there were strains on the finances, I wasn't aware. My parents were unique in their personalities and how they taught us. My mom nurtured us physically and spiritually, as well as intellectually. If we were interested in something, she made sure we had opportunity to try it out and experience it. If we had questions, we could ask and she would give us her answer, her best guess, or help us find out more. She also inspired my love of cooking. She like to try new things and we had a great variety of foods growing up. My dad was the nurturer of our curiosity/exploration. He loves to experience life and all the good that is out there. Whenever we went anywhere, especially somewhere new, we tried new things, went to see all there was to see. I still love going new places, just to experience the atmosphere, a new food, or an old food done by someone new, to see all there is to see, and to learn about it. He also taught me to stay busy, get things done. Both my parents were great at that. Whatever the task at hand, just jump in and get it done.

I have a friend I met when I moved to Alaska who took me under her wing. She helps and encourages me in all my crazy endeavors. She adopted my kids when they came along, and still, many years later does nice things for me and for them. She taught me the importance of thanking people. If I helped her, there was always a thank you, whether it was a note card in the mail, or a small package the next time I saw her. I don't do as good as she always does, but I am more aware of the need to be grateful directly to others because of her example to me.

Several of my kids had the same 2nd grade teacher in Elementary school that I will be forever grateful for. I have a couple kids with anxiety, and they hated to go to school. They had wonderful teachers, but they dreaded going every day. But, this teacher was a phenomenal teacher, and had a structure in her classroom that any and every student could thrive in. My kids did begin to thrive, and learned that school wasn't so bad after all. They have excelled in their academics ever since, and I trace the success of the two with anxiety, in particular, back to this teacher and how she taught.

I have awesome in-laws. I married an awesome man, but he started out awesome because he, like me, was raised by good parents. I was 18 when I got married and had a lot of growing up still to do. But they always gave me the benefit of the doubt, instructed me when I needed help, and supported me as I figured out who I was and who I wanted to be. I am grateful for their good influence on my kids. I am grateful that they have had grandparents right down the road that have loved them unconditionally. They have been an influence for good in our whole family's life.

I couldn't end without sharing how grateful I am for my awesome husband. He supports me in everything I do. When we started our family, it was important to both of us that I stay home and raise our kids. He has worked hard to support our family on one income. As our kids get older and I have started my own business and worked from home, initially spending way more than I was making, he still supported me and allowed me that time and money to try to get things off the ground. I think he does look forward to the day when I do more than just break even as he gets older! We have always felt it was important to teach our kids how to work. With his business, the kids have had plenty of opportunity to work on a job. But he also makes sure they know how to fix things they break, including making repairs to sheetrock, fixing things that break on the cars, proper use of tools, sanding and painting for hours, etc. I am grateful for his dedication to our family, and to educating our kids in the little things that help them become better adults.

I hope you have been thinking about the people in your life who have had an impact for the better on you. Below you will find space to write these people down, and possibly why they have had an impact. I would also encourage you to pick one of those names and send them a note, a text, an email. Something to let them know how grateful you are for them.

1._____

_____

2._____

_____

3._____

_____

4._____

_____

5._____

_____

6._____

_____

7._____
_____

8._____
_____

9._____
_____

10._____
_____

Chapter 5

Physical

I am so grateful for my physical body. But it's funny how sometimes we don't really think about the various parts of our body until something happens to one part, or something goes wrong. Then, we really understand how important our body, or that part of our body is. I remember when I started running, I read an article about an Olympic runner. He said something to the effect that he learned more about his body when he was injured than he ever did when it was easy running, and even though it was hard, he looked back, grateful for those injuries because he had to stop and look at what needed to be done to care for his body better. I have found that to be the case with me as well, not just physically, but in all aspects of my life. When things are going well, we often forget to look at the good and be grateful. It's not until something happens to us that we realize how good it was.

I am going to relate a couple of incidents from my life that reminded me to be grateful more often, and as I do, I want you to think about things that have happened to you physically that have helped you to be grateful for your body and your abilities.

I love playing basketball. I was never courageous enough to try out for my high school basketball team, but I played with our church team. When I was a teenager that was fairly competitive as well, or maybe it was just in the area I grew up in. But it was fun. One day, I can't remember if it was practice or a game, I caught the ball, but it hit my middle finger on my right hand pretty hard. I had jammed my fingers before, and assumed that's what it was. However, it didn't just pull out and feel better. It swelled up and hurt to bend my finger more than normal. My mom took me to the doctor and they x-rayed it. None of the bones were broken, but a piece of the middle knuckle had chipped off and was floating in my finger. It wasn't serious as long as the piece didn't float into the joint, so the doctor splinted it and told me I had to leave it like that for a couple of weeks. He said my body would eventually just absorb the piece of bone floating, and build out the area where it had chipped off. I am right-handed and not at all ambidextrous. I was a serious note taker in high school because I had found that if I wrote it down, I wouldn't forget it. But with the splint on, I couldn't write hardly at all. I also play the piano, and a splinted right hand creates a huge problem in that area. I learned through that experience to be grateful for working hands, and especially fingers. I was so grateful when I could finally take that splint off!

I enjoy exercising. Over the years I have done a lot of different things to exercise, from videos, to treadmills, to running outside, lifting weights, etc. When I first started to run, I had a treadmill that a friend gave me. It was old and the incline feet were gone so I was running uphill, which is a good workout, but because I was a beginner, I started to have problems with my IT band in my right leg. I didn't understand what it was, and all those people who said running hurts your knees started to feel vindicated in their comments. I even started to question a little bit. But through some research I learned a lot about the IT band and how to stretch and heal it. I didn't want to just stop running because I enjoy running, but I also knew that I needed to learn how to fix it and not have problems with it any more. Instead of quitting, I learned. I am so grateful for the information I found, as well as all the people who helped me understand rather than just criticize my chosen form of exercise. I learned through that, and a number of other injuries through the years, to be so grateful for several parts of my body. For my legs that get me everywhere I go, for feet and the role they play in balance, propulsion, and the health of my back, and for the muscles and tendons in my legs that make moving possible.

I have had so many experiences in my life that have made me grateful for my body and the physical things I can do. From breaking my fibula and learning I would much rather break a bone than strain tendons and ligaments. To giving birth and witnessing the incredible power of the female body in its ability to grow another human being, give birth to it, and then recover and become strong again. I have been ever so grateful for my immune system and its ability to fight off the varieties of bacteria and viruses that plague us as humans. My heart that pumps the blood that keeps me alive, and my nervous system that makes literally everything else function. My brain that can learn and grow and understand and my digestive system that keeps everything fed and functioning in a healthy way.

As you can see from above there is so much to our physical being to be grateful for. And when things aren't functioning properly, it helps us to put into perspective how important they are and be more grateful for them when they do. I hope you have been thinking of things you are grateful for and now have at least a couple of them to write down. Below you will find space to write these down. I encourage you to be very specific and try to come up with at least 10 things. You don't have to come up with them all right now, but I hope eventually you will fill in all 10, and even come up with more throughout your life. Look back at them often so that you can remember what your body does for you, and the physical things you are grateful for.

1._____

_____

2._____

_____

3._____

_____

4._____

_____

5._____

_____

6._____

_____

7._____

_____

8._____

_____

9._____

_____

10._____

_____

Chapter 6

Spiritual

This one is a bit harder to define. For me, it is everything that I am grateful for, that has to do with my religion. But if you are not religious, it could be the karma type things, or the positive consequences associated with the things you do. It could possibly be that you notice the changes in you that you have been striving to make. For me, all these are spiritually inclined because my beliefs are so intertwined in who I am. Not that I am perfect, but that all good things that I see, all good things that happen in my life, are a direct result of blessings from my Heavenly Father.

Because this one is a little bit harder to define individually, I will share a few experiences I have had that help me to see that my Heavenly Father is aware of me and my circumstances, and that He cares about where I am going and how I get there. I am grateful for my Heavenly Father, His Son, Jesus Christ, and the opportunity I have to have the Holy Ghost as a constant companion in my life when I strive to live according to Heavenly Father's laws. So many times, in my life I have had the Spirit whisper instructions, pour out knowledge, or help me in times of trouble. I see Him in the details of my life. I want you to think about either those type of experiences you've had, or think of the ways your life is better in any aspect because you have tried to have a positive impact, to serve or help others, or because you have tried to better your life through goal setting and accomplishment.

This first experience is the most recent, but it was orchestrated by the Lord over a year and a half in advance. I realized in late 2019 that my daughters would only have one more Girls' Camp together, and that I had never had the opportunity to go with them to their girls' camps. I wanted to be able to, so I prayed and asked Heavenly Father for that opportunity, if it was His will, to allow me to do so. Well, we all know what happened in 2020 - and girls' camp was cancelled. I was a bit disappointed, but sometimes things don't work out and that's ok. I forgot about it. Roll around to February/March 2021 and I was pulled aside and asked if I would be willing to be the Girls' Camp Director that year for our ward. I was ecstatic! My oldest wasn't in young women's anymore, but I could go with my younger daughter for her last camp. Well, true to the Lord's ability to be in the details of our lives, my oldest daughter decided to go on a mission for our Church. She came home and had the opportunity to serve with me as an Assistant Camp Director in the evenings, while attending her home MTC training for her mission during the day. There is no way that I could ever have imagined after 2020 that I would have the entirety of my prayer fulfilled in such a distinct way. I am grateful for that experience, to be able to see it from start to finish, and for the reminder that the Lord is acutely aware of my circumstances, the righteous desires of my heart, and that nothing is impossible for Him.

The second experience happened not too long ago as well while I was teaching early morning seminary. I have a

20-minute drive from my house to the seminary building. I live in Alaska, so of course, during the school year it is winter almost the entire school year. Driving conditions are often not super great in the early morning, and getting there is sometimes quite the adventure. This particular morning it was snowing where I live, but about 10 miles south it turned to slush falling from the sky, and about 3 miles past that it was freezing rain. I was going slower than the speed limit, but not particularly slow when I had the thought occur to me that semi-truck drivers know the conditions of the road. I have never really thought that true, as they usually go much faster than I consider safe most of the time. Well, that particular morning I found the thought curious, and within a minute I was approaching a semi that was going very slow. I decided to heed that particular warning and let off the gas to start slowing down. I was down to about 30 miles per hour and still moving faster than the semi, so I hit my brakes, just a little bit. I started sliding sideways. The vehicles in front of me were doing the same thing, and it became apparent very quickly just how bad the roads were. Fortunately, we managed to coast down to about 15-20 miles per hour, and we made it safely, all be it late, to seminary that morning. But I was so grateful for that brief warning, the ability to slow without braking for the most part because I was warned early, and for the ability to arrive safely.

I have anxiety. I didn't realize what it was growing up, and I try my best not to let it get the best of me. But there have been times when my kids have been off doing their own thing, with school, sports, or just hanging out with friends, when I haven't been able to get a hold of them. This is terrifying to me, or it used to be. Over the years I have been so grateful for the peace that the Spirit has brought as I pray for help, pray for that child, and ask for understanding or simply ask for confirmation that they are still alive somewhere! Over the years I have learned how to hear better, and to trust no matter what. I am grateful for my Heavenly Father's help, and for the strength to trust. That's really hard sometimes. I am now super grateful for those experiences all these previous years, as my kids are starting to leave home. My oldest daughter is on her mission, and I have complete trust in Heavenly Father's will concerning her and all the missionaries. I am grateful that I have been able to come to that point with her, and I know that I can get to that point with each one of my kids, as it seems to be kid/situation sensitive as to how much anxiety I feel.

I hope as you have read these experiences, that you have thought about how the Lord has had a hand in your life. How have you been blessed by being the help that someone else needed, or by listening to that little voice in your head that speaks to us as we are willing to listen and heed. These experiences are what I call "Tender Mercies". I write these down on a daily basis, because God really is in the details of our lives. But today, I want you to start with just these few lines in this book. Write down any experiences or thoughts that have had an impact on your life. When this page is full, get another book and keep writing. It's amazing how much our Heavenly Father loves us, and does for us every day.

1._____

_____

2._____

_____

GRATITUDE

3._____

_____

4._____

_____

5._____

_____

6._____

_____

7._____

_____

8._____

_____

9._____

_____

10._____

_____

Chapter 7

Talents

We all have talents and natural abilities. It is really easy to see other's talents and be envious, but we need to be grateful for the talents we have, recognize what they are, and increase our own. Talents aren't just physical things either. I have a friend that is really good at recognizing when people are hurting inside, and she is really compassionate and helpful. Those are not things you can see or measure, except when you're the one hurting and receive the help. That's when you see the value of talents like those. I want you to think about some things you are naturally good at while I tell you about some of my talents. I don't tell you mine so you can compare or so I can brag, but just to get you thinking about your own. First, I will tell you about a couple of talents that are obvious, and how I increase them. Then I will tell you about one that isn't so obvious.

I play the piano. My mom started me in piano lessons when I started kindergarten. My piano teacher lived down the street and around the corner and I would walk to her house every week with my piano books and once a month with my mom's payment for my lessons. I actually started learning to play the organ because we had an organ, but my teacher sold organs and pianos, and we soon got a piano. I switched and never looked back. I still remember the basics, but piano is my preferred instrument. Growing up I didn't practice like I should have, but I don't remember ever really wanting to quit. I love music, so this was a natural extension of that love. But I do remember when piano started to be something I loved rather than a chore or part of a check list to practice. It was when I realized I could play anything I wanted. My piano teacher encouraged me to write my own music, which I didn't really do until I was an adult. She also encouraged me to find music I wanted to play. There was a music store just up the road from our house that I walked to whenever I had extra money, and I would buy a piece of sheet music. I loved being able to play the popular songs I heard on the radio. My talent grew when I started playing what I wanted, challenging myself with each new piece of music. Then I started playing the piano for some Church functions and for Seminary. I enjoyed that, and eventually, when my kids were in school, I played the piano for their school concerts. Sharing my talent increased my talent exponentially. That is where I learned that sharing your talents is one of the best ways to grow your talents.

I love working with my hands. I have developed a number of talents through that love. When my husband and I were first married we were traveling a lot between Utah (my home) and Alaska (his home). We didn't fly however, so I had 5 days of riding in the car worth of time to fill. My mom taught me the basic chain and single crochet just before we left on one of first trips back to Alaska. I bought a couple books about crocheting because I discovered I liked it, and learned to crochet. It started pretty simple, and originally, I thought I would like to make blankets. But on a whim, I purchase a book on making doilies. I gained a new talent, and a huge love of hand-made doilies. I made so many doilies on these trips up and down the Alcan Highway. I loved it. I loved making doilies not just because they are pretty, but also because it was super transportable. I could make them anywhere, and it wasn't hard to pick up where I left off. It didn't require a ton of thread like a blanket did, so it never took up much space. I still make doilies. Usually only one or two a year. But when I need something to keep my hands busy, I still go back to making doilies. I also love the finished product. New books with more challenging doilies, as well as a magazine subscription for a while is how I grew that talent, along with lot, and lots, and lots of time!

I love people. When I was a kid, I didn't really look at this as a talent. But as I have gotten older, I realize that seeing people as people, human beings as human beings, is becoming a lost art. People are so engrossed in themselves and what they want, that they don't even look at others with a desire to know who they truly are. I am not perfect at this talent. I get distracted with stuff I have to do, or want to do, and I used to be quite judgmental, but as I have worked on that I have gotten better at just seeing. But I have been working to increase this talent more recently. I enjoy interacting and listening to people's stories. Everyone comes from such a diverse background. Even people who grew up in what we consider similar circumstances look at life differently. It is fun to get to know people, to know why they think the way they think, and feel the way they feel. I also enjoy smiling at people. It is amazing how just a little smile or wave can make others feel happy, can visibly lift them from wherever they were to a new, brighter place. Just a smile. That may not seem like a talent, but there are a lot of grumpy people in this world! This talent was conscientiously increased as I worked on judging less and listening more. It's something I still work on today, but I am grateful for the increased capacity to see people more clearly.

Sometimes it's hard to look at ourselves and see talents, and even harder to appreciate the talents we have because we see so many people better at it than us. But it's not about comparing, it's about seeing ourselves clearly and appreciating what we can do, no matter how "good" we are at it at any given point in time. We see, especially with social media today, everything everyone else is doing, everything they are good at, and we want to be "perfect" like they are. But we don't see two things. One, we don't see the imperfections in everything else around that person. What we see on social media is simply a snapshot that was usually orchestrated to look perfect. And two, we don't take the time to put the phone down and really look at ourselves, the beauty that is us. So, think today about what you are good at, inside or out. What kinds of things do you enjoy doing, what do you want to learn about (those could be hidden talents waiting to be uncovered!). Write these things down and add to the list regularly. Be kind to yourself and your evaluation. None of your talents have to be the best there is, or better than anyone else. I know a lot of people who play the piano better than I do, who paint better and have more experience, who love people just as much or more perfectly than I do. You do your talents in a way that is uniquely you. Embrace and be grateful, then go out and share those talents with others.

1._____

_____

2._____

_____

3._____

_____

4._____

_____

5._____

_____

6._____

_____

7._____

_____

8._____

_____

9._____

_____

10._____

_____

Chapter 8

Keep Going

I hope that as you have gone through this book you have looked at your life with a new perspective, a new appreciation for everything from the world around you, to things that make up you. Being grateful changes our perspectives and helps us see the good in the world, and the good in our own lives. But it does take a conscious effort to be so. I encourage you not to stop here. Take time on a daily basis to write down at least one thing you are grateful for. Write it down and keep it where you can see it, whether in a book you can review, or maybe just a sticky note on your mirror or fridge. I love to look back at the things I have written down over the years. It's a nice walk down memory lane and a great reminder of things that I have since forgotten. Counting our blessings helps us look on the bright side of life.

This is the end of what I am going to write, but I want you to keep going. The next few pages are for you to continue to write down what you are grateful for in the areas that you have just read about. I encourage you to fill in these pages over the next little while, and then, when they're full, get a new book or journal to keep going. Never stop being grateful!

Intellectual

11.

12.

13.

14.

15.

16.

17.

18.

19._____

_____

20._____

_____

Nature

11._____

_____

12._____

_____

13._____

_____

14._____

_____

15._____

_____

16._____

_____

17._____

_____

18._____

_____

19._____

_____

20._____

_____

People

11._____

_____

12._____

_____

13._____

_____

14._____

_____

15._____

_____

16._____

_____

17._____

_____

18._____

_____

19._____

_____

20._____

_____

Physical

11._____

_____

12._____

_____

13._____

_____

14._____

_____

15._____

_____

16._____

_____

17._____

_____

18._____

_____

19._____

_____

20._____

_____

Spiritual

11._____

_____

12._____

_____

13._____

_____

14._____

_____

15._____

_____

16._____

_____

17._____

_____

18._____

_____

19._____

_____

20._____

_____

Talents

11._____

_____

12._____

_____

13._____

_____

14._____

_____

15._____

_____

16._____

_____

17._____

_____

18._____

_____

19._____

_____

20._____

_____

About Me

Hi, my name is Stephanie Richey. I live in Alaska. I am a wife and mom, as well as an artist, writer, piano player, and I love the outdoors. Most of my time, until recently, has been spent raising kids and helping my husband with his business. As my family has gotten more independent though, I have had a little more time to do some things I wanted to do. In the last 5 or so years I have learned to paint, learned to make a website, and learned a lot about products and blogs. I had the opportunity to write a book a few months ago, and felt inspired to write another. Gratitude is a character trait that has blessed my life immensely, and I hope that this book has blessed your life as well.

www.ingramcontent.com/pod-product-compliance
Lightning Source LLC
LaVergne TN
LVHW090054080526
838200LV00082B/4